CH

SandCastle

Sight Words

Just Make Some Art!

Kelly Doudna

Consulting Editor Monica Marx, M.A./Reading Specialist

Publishing Company

Published by SandCastle™, an imprint of ABDO Publishing Company, 4940 Viking Drive, Edina, Minnesota 55435.

Printed in the United States.

Credits
Edited by: Pam Price
Curriculum Coordinator: Nancy Tuminelly
Cover and Interior Design and Production: Mighty Media
Photo Credits: BananaStock Ltd., Brand X Pictures, Comstock, Eyewire Images, Image 100, PhotoDisc

Library of Congress Cataloging-in-Publication Data

Doudna, Kelly, 1963-
    Just make some art! / Kelly Doudna.
       p. cm. -- (Sight words)
    Includes index.
    Summary: Uses simple sentences, photographs, and a brief story to introduce six different words: him, just, make, old, up, would.
    ISBN 1-59197-481-X
    1. Readers (Primary) 2. Vocabulary--Juvenile literature. [1. Reading.] I. Title. II. Series.
PE1119.D67595 2003
428.1--dc21

2003050311

SandCastle™ books are created by a professional team of educators, reading specialists, and content developers around five essential components that include phonemic awareness, phonics, vocabulary, text comprehension, and fluency. All books are written, reviewed, and leveled for guided reading, early intervention reading, and Accelerated Reader® programs and designed for use in shared, guided, and independent reading and writing activities to support a balanced approach to literacy instruction.

Let Us Know

After reading the book, SandCastle would like you to tell us your stories about reading. What is your favorite page? Was there something hard that you needed help with? Share the ups and downs of learning to read. We want to hear from you! To get posted on the ABDO Publishing Company Web site, send us e-mail at:

sandcastle@abdopub.com

SandCastle Level: Beginning

Featured Sight Words

him   just

make   old

up   would

Mick's teacher helps him paint.

Tom just started a new picture.

Ann helps make a big painting.

Jen is six years old.

Sue and Tim do not look up.

Meg would like some help.

Let's Just Paint!

Joe just loves to make art.

He is seven years old.

Amy sits next to him.

She does not look
up.

Joe just finished a painting.

He would like to paint all day.

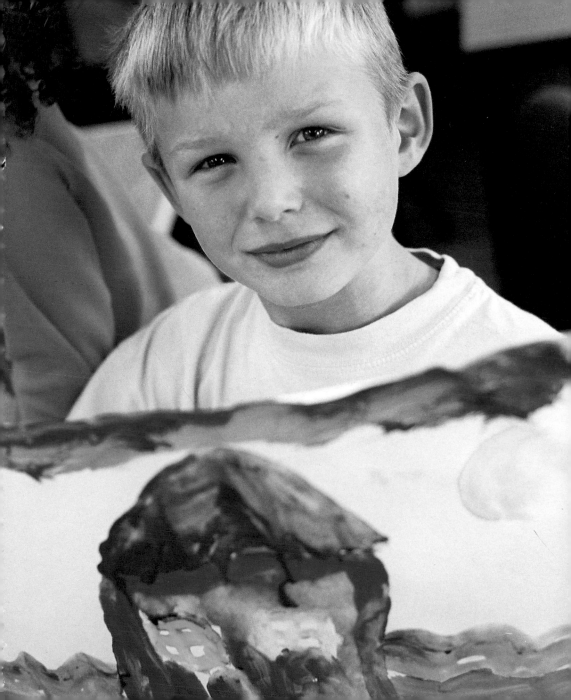

More Sight Words in This Book

a	like
all	new
and	not
day	she
do	some
he	to
is	

All words identified as sight words in this book are from Edward Bernard Fry's "First Hundred Instant Sight Words."

Picture Index

paint, pp. 5, 16, 20

painting, pp. 9, 20

picture, p. 7

seven, p. 16

six, p. 11

teacher, p. 5

About SandCastle™

A professional team of educators, reading specialists, and content developers created the SandCastle™ series to support young readers as they develop reading skills and strategies and increase their general knowledge. The SandCastle™ series has four levels that correspond to early literacy development in young children. The levels are provided to help teachers and parents select the appropriate books for young readers.

Emerging Readers
(no flags)

Beginning Readers
(1 flag)

Transitional Readers
(2 flags)

Fluent Readers
(3 flags)

These levels are meant only as a guide. All levels are subject to change.

To see a complete list of SandCastle™ books and other nonfiction titles from ABDO Publishing Company, visit **www.abdopub.com** or contact us at:

4940 Viking Drive, Edina, Minnesota 55435 • 1-800-800-1312 • fax: 1-952-831-1632